Homesteaders and Indians

This group of men wait at a railroad siding for a train to take them westward, to work harvesting wheat. Many of them were homesteaders who needed money to help them through a bad season or their first years on a claim. The flatcar is loaded with farm machinery. Telegraph lines run along the railroad. The telegraph was almost as important as the railroad in the opening of the West. Indians knew how important the telegraph was in sending messages fast. They often attacked railroads and telegraph lines — tearing up tracks and chopping down poles. .

Homesteaders and Indians

by Dorothy Levenson

illustrated with photographs and contemporary drawings

←A FIRST BOOK→

Franklin Watts, Inc.
845 Third Avenue
New York, N.Y. 10022

Photographs courtesy of:

With the following exceptions, all photographs were provided through the courtesy of the Library of Congress or the New York Public Library.
Nebraska State Historical Society: page 47
New York State Museum and Science Service: page 30
Smithsonian Institution: page 71 (top)

THE PICTURES IN THIS BOOK

The pictures in this book are drawings or photographs made during the nineteenth century, when the settlers were moving westward. Many of them appeared in newspapers and magazines published in New York or Boston. Readers were interested in stories about the homesteaders and the Indians. Many of them had relatives out west or were thinking of going there themselves.

Photography was still very complicated. Nineteenth-century cameras could not take clear pictures of anything moving. Photographs could not be easily reproduced. Magazines and newspapers employed artists to draw pictures for them. Sometimes these artists copied photographs, sometimes they went out west to see for themselves, and sometimes they used their imaginations. .

SBN 531-00734-0
Copyright © 1971 by Franklin Watts, Inc.
Library of Congress Catalog Card Number: 79-136832
Printed in the United States of America

2 3 4 5

Contents

Homesteaders and Indians

Fur traders were often the first white men that Indians met. These fur traders with their boat loaded with bundles of furs are being attacked by Indians on the Missouri River. In many cases fur traders lived peacefully among Indians for years. Many of them married Indian women, and their children suffered during the Indian wars.

The Long War

For thousands of years the land that is now the United States belonged to the people we call Indians. They spoke many different languages. They lived in many different ways. Some were farmers. Some were hunters. Some lived deep in the forests in villages of strongly built houses. Others roamed over the grassy plains, carrying all they owned with them.

Each Indian belonged to a tribe, which was made up of a number of bands. Just two or three families made up some bands. Each Indian thought of himself first not as one man but as part of a band and of a tribe. All the members of a band took care of each other. They hunted or fished or farmed together and shared whatever they caught or grew.

Some tribes were warlike. Others lived in peace.

Indian religions were many. Some believed in one god, others in many, but all believed that man and nature were very close. Hunters or farmers all knew that the wind, the rain, the sun, the grass, the trees, and all the animals that lived on earth were important to them. Indians did not believe that any man or group of men could own the land. The sky, the air, and the earth belonged to everyone. A tribe might think of a particular area over which they traveled or a place where they grew corn as their territory but they did not think they owned that land.

"Sell land!" said the great Indian leader Tecumseh. "As well sell air and water. The Great Spirit gave them in common to all."

For thousands of years Indians wandered through the for-

3

ests, over the grassy plains and great deserts. The earth was their mother, supplying all their wants. Then men arrived from Europe, men who wanted to take this land and have it for their own. These men believed that land could be cut up and bought and sold.

In 1513 the Spaniard Ponce de Leon arrived in Florida. He did not stay, but he was followed by other Europeans who came to settle the land that was to become the United States. Spaniards came and Frenchmen came. Settlers came from England to Virginia and Massachusetts. Dutchmen founded the city of New Amsterdam on the island of Manhattan. For hundreds of years men sailed from Europe to the land where the Indians had roamed free.

These settlers wanted the Indians' land. They wanted it for farms. They wanted land on which to build their cities. They cut down the forests and plowed the earth. Sometimes they bought land from the Indians. Sometimes they made treaties with the Indians in which it was agreed that part of the land belonged to the newcomers and part to the Indians. As more men came from Europe, there were more men who wanted Indian land. The Indians could not sell or give away all their land, but the settlers wanted it all.

The Indians fought for their land. They went on fighting for almost four hundred years. But they did not fight as one people — the Indians were never able to unite. They continued to speak many languages. And each Indian continued to think of himself as the member of a tribe, not as the member of one Indian nation. During the years of fighting, the tribes were at war with each other as well as with the settlers from Europe.

At first the tribes had only bows and arrows and spears as

weapons. The Europeans had guns. Later the Indians were able to buy guns, but they could never afford to support a full-time army or buy the best weapons. An Indian warrior always had to spend most of his time hunting and caring for his family and members of his band and tribe.

The United States Against the Indians

In the late eighteenth century the settlers in the thirteen colonies on the east coast joined together to form the United States. They drove out the British and turned to fight the Indians for possession of the land between the Allegheny Mountains and the Pacific Ocean.

From the beginning, the United States government knew that the Indians would have to be conquered. Indian affairs were placed under the War Department until 1849, when the Department of the Interior took charge of Indian matters, with the army always ready to help. The new nation was always able to support a well-equipped professional army.

Although the United States was a new nation, it was much stronger than any Indian tribe. English was the official language, and most new immigrants learned it. All people who arrived in the United States came to think of themselves as Americans.

Most new settlers believed that land could be owned and bought and sold. And many of them thought that land should be available to whoever wanted it; that any new settler, however poor, should be able to own his own farm.

Again and again, citizens of the United States, especially settlers in the West, asked the government to give them free land.

Few people stopped to think that Indians had any right to this land. Few white men, indeed, thought of Indians as people with rights at all. Most citizens of the United States thought of

people with skins of a color different from their own as being inferior. White settlers from Europe bought black men, women, and children from Africa as slaves. They called Indians redskins; they tried and failed to enslave them and said they were uncivilized.

Indians were driven out of their homes in the eastern United States. Thousands of men, women, and children were marched hundreds of miles from their homes in Georgia to Oklahoma. The Cherokee Indians appealed to the United States Supreme Court to protect them. The Supreme Court agreed that the Cherokees should be allowed to stay in their misty mountain homes, but President Jackson defied the Supreme Court. The

Cherokees were driven out along the "Trail of Tears" to Oklahoma. Thousands died on the way. In Florida the United States fought two long wars with the Seminoles.

Indians were deported. Indians were killed. By the middle of the nineteenth century the white settlers had spread all the way to the Mississippi River. But the United States was a country with its own deep divisions. The North was a land of farms and cities where free men worked. The white settlers in the South, however, owned millions of black slaves. These slaves worked on the great plantations owned by the white settlers.

Congressmen from Southern states had never been sure that land should be given away. The idea of "free land" and slavery did not seem to go together. They wanted the West to be filled by large plantations worked by slaves, not by small farms owned by free men.

In 1861, civil war broke out between the North and the South. The Southern states seceded to form their own country, the Confederate States of America. Men from the North now controlled Congress. At last they were able to pass a law to give free land to any settler who wanted it. The Homestead Act of 1862 said that anyone who was twenty-one years old or the head of a family could be given 160 acres of land. The offer was open to any citizen of the United States or anyone who had declared that he was going to become a citizen. The only money a farmer had to pay out was a small "filing fee" to cover the cost of registering his land.

The law brought hope to millions of poor people that someday they would be able to own their own farms. Men toiling in the cities of the East dreamed of being independent on their own land. Farmers struggling in the stony fields of New England

Settlers banded together in wagon trains for company and protection as they crossed the prairies. Many black men traveled westward as settlers or cowboys, looking for the freedom and safety they could not find in the South.

heard of the fertile lands of the West. Men who had gone west looking for gold decided that farming might be a surer way of making a living. In Europe, men dreamed of freedom and free land in the United States. Once the war ended in 1865, soldiers who had served in the Northern and Southern armies headed west. In the South, millions of black people who had once been slaves were free. Many of them felt that the Homestead Act gave them a way to support their families.

One group of people who were not pleased by the Homestead Act were the Indians. Many of them were living on the land that Congress was giving to the farmers.

More than half of the United States was still home to the Indian and the buffalo. California and Oregon had been settled by farmers and miners, but most of the wide land from the Missouri to the Rockies had never been plowed. Vast herds of buffalo roamed the grassy plains. Indian tribes followed the buffalo, hunting them for food and skins.

Both the Indians who had lived on the prairies for thousands of years and those like the Cherokees who had been sent west by the United States government wondered what was going to happen.

Across the Wide Missouri

Most of the land opened for settlement by the Homestead Act lay between the Missouri River and the Rocky Mountains. This is a wide-open land. Blizzards sweep across the treeless prairies in winter. Blazing sun beats down in summer. For many years men called much of this land the Great American Desert. They thought the prairies were too dry for farming.

There were many different Indian tribes living on the Great Plains. Some were farmers, but most of the Plains Indians were wanderers who spent their time following the great herds of buffalo. Millions of buffalo roamed the prairies. Buffalo meat was the chief food of the Plains Indians. Furry buffalo robes kept them warm in winter. Buffalo skins were used to make clothing to wear and tents in which to live.

These Indian families lived in tepees made by putting up frames of straight poles over which buffalo skins were stretched. In the top there was a hole through which the smoke from the cooking fire could escape. Inside, the family slept on buffalo robes.

Once the Plains Indian hunted buffalo on foot. When the tribe moved, everything they owned had to be packed — tepees, robes, clothing, cooking pots. All their belongings were piled on wooden frames and dragged along by dogs that were harnessed to the frames.

For hundreds of years white men had been visiting the plains to meet and trade with Indians. Explorers and trappers came on horseback. Indian tribes found runaway horses — or stole

To make a tepee, first a framework of straight poles was built. The poles were hard to collect on the treeless paririe. As many as ten people might live in a tepee. The iron pot over the fire, hanging from an iron frame, as well as the other cooking pots and the plaid blankets, must have come from white traders. The wagon must also have come from the white man, since no Indians used wheels for transportation.

them. Soon all the Plains Indians rode horses. They could follow the buffalo farther. Because horses could carry heavier loads than dogs, tepees could be larger and each family could carry more clothing and blankets.

Indian tools were made from wood or stone. An ax had a wooden handle and a stone head tied on with strips of buffalo hide. This hide was tied while wet. As it dried it shrank, became tight, and held the ax head firmly. Arrowheads were made of stone. When white fur traders came to the plains, the Indians traded furs for metal tools — steel axes, arrowheads, and guns.

Spoons and cups were made from buffalo horn. An Indian housewife used bags made from buffalo skin to carry food and she used buffalo sinews as sewing thread.

Wood for cooking fires was scarce on these treeless prairies. Indian children collected buffalo chips — dry buffalo manure — to feed the supper fire.

Most clothing was made from buffalo skin or deerskin. In the hot summer, children often wore nothing at all and men wore just a breechcloth. Women wore deerskin dresses and leggings up to their knees. In cold weather, men wore long pants and everyone used furry buffalo robes to keep warm.

Both men and women decorated their clothes for special occasions. Some men's shirts were covered in designs made with paint or beads or porcupine quills. Women decorated their best dresses with beads or quills or elk's teeth.

Buffalo fur grew heavier in winter. The fur from buffalo killed then was used to make mittens, caps, and moccasins, all lined with the warm fur. The buffalo killed at other times of the year did not have such thick fur. Those skins were used for

13

shirts and dresses and leggings. The delicate skin of buffalo calves was thin enough to make into underwear.

After a hunt the whole tribe feasted on fresh buffalo meat roasted over an open fire. The meat that was not eaten then was preserved and stored for the long months ahead. The women cut strips of buffalo meat and dried them in the sun. They pounded the dry meat with a stone hammer, mixed it with buffalo fat and berries, and packed the mixture, called pemmican, into bags of buffalo skin to keep until it was needed.

Indian women worked hard. They cooked and prepared all the food. After the men had killed a buffalo, the women skinned it, cut up the meat, and tanned the skins so that they could be used to make tepees or clothes. The women made all the family clothes. They also gathered wild roots and berries for the tribe to eat or grew the food if their tribe did some farming.

The hard-riding buffalo hunters of the Great Plains became the most famous Indians of all, but in the drier areas of the West poorer bands of Indians roamed. They lived on what they could gather or hunt — berries and nuts, lizards and birds and prairie dogs. In the Northwest, between the Rocky Mountains and the Cascade Mountains, were rivers full of fish. Many Indian tribes built permanent villages along the banks of these rivers. Indians of the Southwest also lived in permanent towns, farming the country around them.

In all, these Indians added up to less than a million people

Plains Indians became great horsemen. An Indian warrior could shoot a bow and arrow while riding a galloping horse — or he could swing down to one side and hide behind the body of his horse as it raced along. This Indian warrior is dressed as many Indian men were in warm weather — just in moccasins and breechcloth.

This Indian man and his wife are dressed in a combination of styles. Her dress is of buffalo skins but she has on white knitted stockings (or long underwear). He wears moccasins and his hair is Indian fashion, but his shirt, pants, and vest probably came from a trading post.

divided into many tribes speaking many different languages. By 1860, the population of the United States was over thirty million. The Indians were not citizens of the United States. The government had declared: "The Indians residing within the United States are so far independent that they live under their own customs and not under the laws of the United States, that their rights upon the lands which they inhabit or hunt are secured to them by boundaries defined in amicable treaties between the United States and themselves."

The United States was so much stronger than the Indians that treaties usually favored the United States. The biggest problem that the Indians had with treaties, however, was that they were broken. Indians were constantly finding that lands guaranteed to them "forever" were given to white settlers. Almost as soon as a treaty was signed, the United States asked for more land. Often the government agreed to pay for land in yearly installments of goods — food and guns, blankets and axes. Indian agents were sent to make these payments to the tribes. Sometimes the agents were dishonest. Sometimes the government changed its mind about the amount of the payment. Many times, when the Indians came to collect, they found that the payment was not as large as had been agreed upon. This could mean disaster if a tribe had been depending upon supplies

Homesteaders put great pressure on Congress to open up the Indian lands of Oklahoma to settlement. These lands had been given "forever" to the Indians who had been moved there from the East. A date and time were given for the opening of the "Cherokee Strip." Settlers lined up in covered wagons and on horseback. The signal was given and settlers raced for their land claims.

from the agent to feed its people during the winter. Many attacks made by Indians upon settlers began because the agent had not given the Indians all the food and blankets they had expected.

In many of the treaties the tribes agreed to live on particular pieces of land called reservations. Often reservations started out very large but, like the payments from the agent, they had a habit of shrinking. When the Cherokees and other tribes were moved from the eastern United States they were given almost the whole of what is now the state of Oklahoma as a reservation. There they settled down to farming. The Oklahoma Indians made the mistake of siding with the South in the Civil War. As punishment, half their land was taken away. Gradually, more and more of the land remaining was taken away until in the end most of Oklahoma was owned by white settlers.

The Homesteaders

The men who came west to take up land under the Homestead Act did not think of themselves as taking land from the Indians. Most of them were men who had worked all their lives as farmers. They came west to find good land. Many of them came from other parts of the United States — from Illinois or Wisconsin or New England. Some came because their farms were poor and they wanted better land. Some came because they were the sons of farmers and there was no room for them on the family farm. There were black settlers from the South who had been slaves and now were farmers without land. Homesteaders came from Europe — especially from Norway, Sweden, and Germany. In crowded Europe it was hard for a poor man to buy land. In the empty spaces of the West they could find room for themselves and their children.

At the end of the Civil War there were no roads that went all the way across the United States and no railroad that went all the way west. Many settlers traveled by covered wagon. Curved wooden bows were fitted over a flat wagon and canvas was stretched across this to make a roof. The family set up a cookstove in the middle of the wagon, with a pipe for smoke poking through the top. Everything that a family needed for the journey that took months was packed into the wagon. So were the plow and all the tools and seeds to start the new farm.

As homesteaders got ready for the long journey, they thought carefully about what they planned to take along. Years might pass before they would have a chance to buy new supplies. How

Many families went westward in covered wagons, sometimes pulled by horses, sometimes by oxen.

they packed was also important. After seventy years one family still remembered a bottle of ink a boy put into the wagon — it leaked along the way and spoiled his sister's clothes. Flour, sugar, beans, and salt pork all had to be packed. Blankets and sheets and clothes for the family, including diapers for the baby, were folded away.

Oxen or horses pulled the wagons. The cow followed along and so did the dog. Mother and the smaller children rode in the bumpy wagon. Father and the older children walked the whole way. Every night the family camped and mother cooked supper. Morning and evening the cow was milked. The cream was put in a pail and hung under the wagon. The jolting of the wagon turned the cream to butter.

Often the whole wagonload had to wait because one of the animals had sore feet or one of the family was sick. Mother insisted on stopping once in a while so that she could do the family wash. Father took a day off to go hunting for fresh meat to feed his family.

Groups of families joined together to form wagon trains. In that way, families could help each other in time of trouble or band together to fight off an Indian attack.

Railroads

Before many years had passed, travelers had other ways of going west. The age of homesteading was also the age of railroads. The first railroad to go right across the country was finished in 1869. Soon two more cross-country lines were finished. In 1860 there were 30,000 miles of railroads in the United States. Forty years later there were several times as many.

Railroads and settlers moved west together. The homesteaders wanted to reach their land and then to send their crops to market. They were cash-crop farmers. The homesteaders farmed land where often only one thing grew well — corn or wheat or cattle. They had to buy many of the things a family needed. The railroads brought supplies to the lonely little Western towns and took the wheat and cattle east to market.

The government knew that railroads were important to the country and helped the railroad builders by lending them money and giving them land. Millions of acres on which to build their lines were given to railroad companies. Other millions of acres were given to the companies to sell so that they could raise money to pay for the cost of laying their lines. The railroad companies sold this land to settlers.

Indeed, there were complaints that the railroads were given too much land or given all the best land. Settlers also said that the rates the railroads charged to take their crops to market were too high. They asked the federal government to control the railroad companies as well as help them.

The Indian tribes soon saw that the railroads threatened

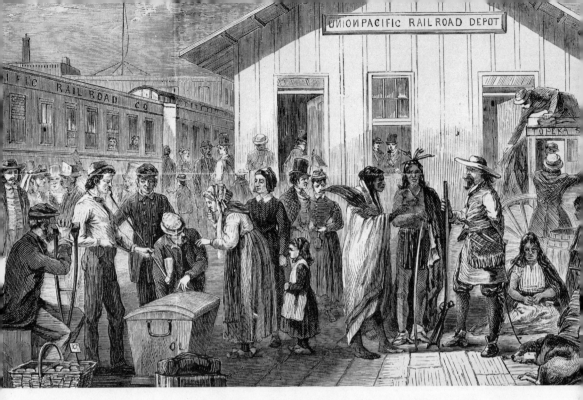

A railroad station was a busy place. All the variety of people who came west are here at the Union Pacific Railroad Depot at Omaha City, Nebraska. There are black men and white men. There is a family in wooden shoes who came all the way from Holland. There are Indians with a baby in a carrying frame. There is a hunter with his gun and knife and broad hat. There is a gentleman in a top hat with a lady carrying a parasol. The stagecoach waits for passengers. Once people left the railroad they traveled by coach, on horseback, or on foot.

them. The noisy trains frightened the buffalo and other animals. And the railroads could bring in many more settlers than could the slow lines of covered wagons. The Indians attacked the men laying the tracks. They tore up tracks once they were laid and even attacked the locomotives when they started puffing their way across the plains.

The trains that immigrants rode were not very comfortable. This train has wooden seats and wooden sleeping platforms on top. Travelers carried their own pillows and blankets. They could bring their own food or buy it at stops along the way. Pets came along, too.-

Nothing stopped the railroads. Special "immigrant" trains ran to take settlers west. Railroads advertised for settlers. They took newspaper reporters on trips across the country so that the reporters would go home and write stories in their local papers about the beautiful land out west. The railroad companies even sent men to Europe to persuade people to come to the United States.

Sod Houses and Claim Shanties

The land onto which the homesteaders moved was different from land in the eastern United States. Pioneers in the East found the land covered with forests. The first thing a settler did was to cut down trees. That was hard work but he could use the trunks of the trees to build a log cabin for his family. In the great forests there were always trees to cut for firewood. Settlers could cook and keep their families warm.

As homesteaders moved across the Missouri River they found that this was a land of little rain and few trees. Much of the country was flat prairie covered with thick grass. A man could look for miles and see only the prairie grasses waving in the wind. Cottonwoods grew along riverbanks, but their wood was soft, and a cabin built of cottonwood rotted quickly.

As soon as a farmer reached his claim he thought about putting up a house, for his family had to have somewhere to live. Even more important, the law said that there had to be a house "twelve by fourteen" on the claim. Not all homesteaders were honest. They wanted land not to live on but to sell for a profit. They might put up a toy house — twelve by fourteen inches, not twelve by fourteen feet. But most settlers built real houses.

Where there were no trees at all, homesteaders learned to build their houses of sod cut from the prairie. Here in the West a man began to build a house by plowing half an acre of ground. His plow turned up thick sod, earth, grass, and roots, matted together. He cut this up in pieces and used these pieces of sod as if they were bricks. First he marked out the plan of his house

A sod house. Wood was used for the door frames and window frames. This house even has glass windows. There is a shady place to eat out of doors and a pump for the water supply.

with one row of sod, leaving a space where the door was to be. He built up the walls with sod, filling up the cracks with earth. From pieces of wood he made a door frame and a window frame. He put these in place and built up the sod around them. If he found hickory wood, he built strips of it into the walls to make them stronger.

A roof was difficult to build up. At each end of the house the settler stood a forked pole and laid another pole across these. The poles were the frame for the roof. Poles and brushwood and grass were laid over these, and on top of all was placed a layer of sod. The cracks in the sod roof were filled with earth. Soon the roof of a sod house had its own cover of grass and flowers sprouting in the sod.

Some families made their homes, at least temporarily, in dugouts on a riverbank or the side of a hill. To make this kind of a house the farmer dug a cave in the bank and built a front wall from sod.

The thick walls made sod houses cool in summer and warm in winter, but made them dark. Not much air or sunlight could get in. The settler's wife found that she could not keep a sod house clean. She sprinkled her dirt floor with water to try to keep the dust down. If rain came the roof was soaked and muddy water dripped all over everyone.

A few families became fond of their sod houses. They plastered the inside walls with clay and whitewashed them. They bought good furniture and moved it into the sod house.

Most wives, however, were glad to leave their dark and dusty houses. They moved into a wooden house as soon as their husbands could afford to buy the wood to build one. The family's old sod house often became a barn for the cows and horses.

The lack of trees meant there was no wood to burn in the fires for cooking. Settlers learned to use the same fuel as the Indians — buffalo chips. The farm children, like the Indian children, were sent out to gather buffalo chips. If a cattle drive went through, the children were sent to collect the droppings left by the Texas longhorns.

If he did not build a sod house, a farmer built a "claim

shanty" of rough boards bought in one of the little towns. Wood was expensive to buy because it had to be brought from far away. The shanties were small and they were not as cool in the summer as sod houses. The hot prairie sun beat down on the bare boards and tar-paper roof, for there were no trees around to provide shade. Water was too precious to be used for growing flowers. Housewives threw the water in which they washed clothes or dishes in the yard outside the shanty door. This kept down the dust. The soap in the water soaked into the earth so that nothing could grow there.

In winter a claim shanty was not as warm as a sod house. The cold winds whistled through the boards. Settlers tried to keep their shanties warm by piling earth against the outside walls. When the temperature went down below zero anything in the shanty could freeze. The farmer burned buffalo chips to keep warm. He twisted strands of hay together to make sticks to burn. There was constant danger of freezing. The precious seed potatoes he was saving to plant in the spring might freeze. The farmer often took them to bed with him to keep them warm. Families burned their few sticks of furniture to keep from freezing. Unlucky farmers froze to death alone in their shanties on the great cold prairie.

People were just beginning to learn that germs cause disease. This picture from a magazine was meant to warn people not to throw dirty water near a well. The water could soak into the ground and pollute the water in the well. Pioneer houses had no indoor plumbing. The water supply came from the well. The outhouse in the back of the picture is the family toilet.

Crops

Once a farmer had built his house he thought about planting a crop. He did not have to spend time cutting trees. He started plowing at once. When he turned over the thick prairie sod the earth was full of grass and roots. Wheat could not fight its way through that. The first crop was usually sod potatoes or sod corn — corn and potatoes could fight their way through that tough prairie grass. The farmer dropped his cut-up potatoes or corn in the earth and covered them with sod. In a year the dead grass and roots rotted and the farmer started growing wheat. In the meantime, his family ate potatoes and corn. They ate baked potatoes and mashed potatoes and boiled potatoes. They ate corn bread, cornmeal, corn pudding, corn on the cob, corn dodgers, and corn gruel. Children carried corn bread and molasses to the one-room schoolhouse for lunch.

The Indians had been growing corn long before the European settlers arrived in America. When the white settlers began moving westward onto Indian lands, corn was one of the most important items in their diet.

The Women of the West

The wife of a homesteader worked hard. She did all the cooking, all the housework, all the cleaning, and helped her husband in the fields too. She made her own soap and candles, in addition to all the family clothes. She saw to it that her family had enough food to last all year. In the fall she stored up the food for her family to eat through the long, cold winter. The prairie housewife froze her meat in the early winter and kept it outdoors in the bitter cold. She dried apples and pumpkins to be used for pies. In the hot summer she struggled to keep food from spoiling with no refrigerator or ice.

The women of the frontier were lonely. They were far from family or friends, and neighbors were often miles away. It took weeks, or even months, for letters to reach home. Women felt especially lonely when they or their children were sick. There were no hospitals and not many doctors. If the crop was bad a man might have to go off and work on the railroad to make money. His wife and children remained at home to protect the claim so that no one could come along and say the land was unoccupied. Staying behind was the loneliest life of all.

In all of the United States at this time women had few rights. They could not vote. They could not serve on juries. There were not many ways in which a woman could earn a living. She could be a servant or a teacher.

Women out west had one advantage. There were more men than women. Many single men became homesteaders or miners or cowboys. A girl who wanted to marry had a large selection of

Housewives made their own butter and much appreciated anything that made their work easier. Advertisements in newspapers and magazines carried news of new products on the market such as cookstoves and sewing machines.

men from which to choose. A homesteader's wife had to work hard, but if her husband mistreated her there were other men ready to protect her. Divorce became popular in the West long before it was accepted in the East. The Homestead Act itself helped women. It did not say "any man" could have a quarter section. The words were "any person." There were women who filed a claim on a piece of land, built a claim shanty, and lived there the five years the law required for the legal ownership.

Many young women became schoolteachers. The settlers were eager for their children to have an education. As soon as there were a few families in an area they banded together to build a one-room schoolhouse and pay the salary of any girl who had enough education to teach.

Little towns grew up around the railroad depots on the prairies and around the mines in the mountains. Women ran boardinghouses, restaurants, and stores in these towns. The miners

Women were allowed to vote for the first time in the United States in the election of 1888 in Wyoming Territory. About thirty years passed before the federal government gave the right to vote to all women in the United States. These women are standing in the snow to vote in Cheyenne. The little boy holds a picnic basket. His mother probably traveled many miles to cast her first vote.

and the farmers and the cowboys needed clothes. Many a woman made a living sewing.

These hardworking women decided that they made just as useful citizens as men and asked for legal rights. It was in these Western states that women were first allowed to vote. As the voters began to organize to make demands on the government and the railroads the women were there with the men. It was a woman who told the men they should "raise more hell and less corn."

Barbed Wire and Sewing Machines

The homesteaders were moving westward at a time when the United States and the whole world were changing rapidly. Machines and the things made by machines were becoming much more important. The last half of the nineteenth century was a time of inventions — the kind of inventions that made living and working easier for ordinary men and women.

All farms needed fences. In the East they were made of wood or stone. On the prairies, where there was not enough of either, barbed wire was the answer. Two strands of wire were twisted together with sharp spikes strung along them at intervals. In 1874, when the first barbed wire was made, a hundred pounds cost twenty dollars. Farmers bought such large quantities that the price went down to about one-tenth of that.

Machines were invented that could plow and reap and bind up the wheat. Using such machines, one man could farm much more land, but reapers and binders were expensive. Groups of farmers banded together to buy them. In some Western states large companies bought huge farms and hired men to raise crops by machine.

In winter the settlers' homes were bitterly cold, but the cold killed the insects. In summer, life was made miserable by the hordes of flies and mosquitoes. Window screens probably brought more comfort to farm families than did any other product of the factories.

This was a time when people, especially women, wore a great deal of clothing. Women's dresses, trimmed with rows and rows

With machinery farmers could handle much larger crops. Early machinery was driven by steam. The large steam engine at the bottom is being used to power the machine that is threshing the wheat. Farmers still needed many horses to pull the machines. Machines meant that large numbers of men worked together to bring in the crop. At the top right, men are gathering the wheat in the fields. At the top left is the grain elevator where the wheat will be stored until taken away by train.

of tucks and buttons, came down to their ankles. Skirts were full, and under them were layers of petticoats. Pale skin was thought to be beautiful. To keep the sun off their faces and avoid getting a suntan, women and girls wore sunbonnets out of doors.

All these clothes were hot and uncomfortable and hard to work in. Worst of all, they had to be made by hand. Women and girls spent all of their "spare time" sewing. The invention of the sewing machine did more than anything else to lighten women's load of work.

The products of the factories — the machines for the farm, the barbed wire, the sewing machines — all cost money. The farmer had to be able to sell his crops or borrow money from the bank to tide him over a bad season.

Many homesteaders had bad luck. They lost their farms as a result of too many dry years. There were droughts that killed all the crops and prairie fires that burned the wheat standing in the fields. Plagues of grasshoppers ate everything green. For some farmers there was nothing to do but go back east. Thousands of others, however, continued to come west. They took up land under the Homestead Act or they bought land from the railroads. The government passed other laws to make it easier to buy land. These pioneers added almost two million farms to the number of farms in the United States.

Bad Times

For many years men argued about the land between the Missouri and the Rockies that some called the Great American Desert. Some said that only Indians knew how to live there. Some said not enough rain fell for crops to grow there.

Other men said there was plenty of rain and that it was wonderful country where anything could grow. There were men who actually believed that "rain follows the plow" — if men farmed the land and planted crops and trees, more rain would fall.

That, of course, was nonsense. The truth was that the land out west was dry, much drier than that in the East. Some crops would grow well and some not at all. New kinds of wheat had to be developed to grow fast in the hot summers.

Some land was good for farming if water could be brought to it. Farmers near rivers irrigated their land by digging ditches for the water to run along. Some farmers dug wells and hauled up water in buckets. In many areas of the West there was water under the ground, but often it was so far down that no man could haul it up in buckets. Many farmers built windmills. When the wind blew — and that was almost all the time on the prairie — the arms of the windmill went round and round. The power hauled up the water.

This water was not enough to water 160 acres. It was enough to give water to the cattle. It was enough to water the vegetable garden. Even if there was not enough rain, the farmer with a windmill and a vegetable garden could feed his family.

The early years of homesteading happened to be years of good

Prairie fires were a great danger in hot summers when dry grass burned quickly. Sparks from wood-burning engines often started fires. A herd of buffalo is stampeding away from the fire.

HARPER'S WEEKLY.

JOURNAL OF CIVILIZATION

Vol. XVIII.—No. 912.]   NEW YORK, SATURDAY, JUNE 20, 1874.   [WITH A SUPPLEMENT. PRICE TEN CENTS.

Entered according to Act of Congress, in the Year 1874, by Harper & Brothers, in the Office of the Librarian of Congress, at Washington.

IRRIGATION IN COLORADO—LETTING WATER INTO A SIDE SLUICE-WAY.—[SEE PAGE 514.]

Some areas of the West did not have much rain but did have rivers. Farmers worked together to bring water to dry land. These farmers have built a long, wooden sluiceway to bring water down the mountain to their farms. They are opening a gate to let water through. .

rainfall. Settlers did not know that there was not always as much rain as that. They moved farther and farther west. There were a few years of good crops, then came the disasters.

Grasshoppers arrived. One morning a settler looked up and saw what seemed to be a cloud covering the sun. This was no ordinary cloud. It seemed to shimmer and glisten. It seemed to be made up of many small parts. The small parts began to fall to the earth. They were grasshoppers. They came down all over the fields. They crawled, they flew. They were everywhere.

After grasshoppers ate up all the crops, families worked together sweeping them up in piles and burning them to clear the fields.
Children went barefoot in summer but everybody wore a hat because being in the sun was thought to be dangerous.

They crawled over the earth. If a door or a window was left open they crawled into the house. They crunched underfoot. They crawled over women's skirts and in their hair. They crawled over sleeping babies.

They were so thick on the ground that trains could not run.

Everywhere they went the grasshoppers ate. People could hear the munching sounds made by those thousands of busy jaws. They ate the corn and the wheat in the fields. They ate the tomatoes and beans in the vegetable gardens. They ate the leaves off the trees. They ate the waving prairie grasses.

Farmers tried to chase them away and to drive them away with smoky fires, but nothing helped. The grasshoppers ate and ate. The only ones who were happy were the farmers' chickens, who feasted on grasshoppers. Thousands of farmers were ruined by the grasshoppers. Many went back east.

After the years of good rain came years of drought. The hot prairie sun beat down month after month. When there was no rain, crops withered and died.

Every winter there were blizzards. The swirling snow and the cold were frightening. A man could be lost and frozen to death between his house and his barn. The worst blizzard of all was in 1886. In late fall, freezing rain came and covered the prairie grass with ice. The cattle could not eat. Then came a winter such as no man could remember. Blizzard after blizzard roared across the plains.

Many farmers died of cold or starvation in their flimsy claim shanties. Some moved into little prairie towns so that there would be neighbors nearby. Trains loaded with supplies could not get through the great snowdrifts.

Many homesteaders headed back east after that winter. Most

42

homesteaders did not have enough money to survive more than one bad year. Even if land was free a man had to have money to buy seed and food and a new plow or the new machinery that was becoming necessary for farming. If a homesteader had no money he had to borrow some from a bank. That was fine if he had a good crop to sell the next year and he could then pay back his bank loan. But if there was not enough rain the next year, that could be the end of the farmer. If he could not repay his loan the farm belonged to the bank.

Black Settlers

Before the Civil War most black people in the United States lived in the South and most of them were slaves. Black men who lived in the North were not entirely free. Many states had laws to keep black people out. At the end of the Civil War the black people were no longer slaves. For a few years black people in both the North and the South hoped and even thought that they were truly free. For a time they looked around and what they saw looked like freedom. Black children were going to school. Black men were able to vote and become members of the government. Black people were free to travel, free to take whatever jobs they could find.

The time of freedom did not last long. Most white Southerners accepted black freedom only because soldiers from the North came south to see that the law was obeyed. In 1877, the Northern soldiers went home and white Southerners took power again. Black men found that the South was not very different from the way it had been under slavery. Laws were passed that said black and white children could not go to school together. Black and white people could not eat together or ride a train together. Black men were not allowed to vote and there were no more black men in government.

White men were able to control the South because they owned most of the land, most of the money, and most of the guns. Black men found it hard to make a living and take care of their families. When they were slaves everything had belonged to their masters — the land they farmed, the food they ate, the clothes they wore. Many dreamed that when they were given freedom they would also be given "forty acres and a mule." When freedom came at last, ex-slaves were given nothing. When the Northern soldiers went home, most black people in the South looked around and saw that they had no land, no mule, no vote, no freedom. They found they often had to go back and work for the man who had owned them before the war. That man was not usually interested in paying his ex-slaves any more or treating them any better than he had before. If a black man tried to argue about wages or anything else, he would find himself — or his wife or his children — being beaten or even killed.

To many blacks it seemed that the West might be a better place to live than the South. Before the war, Benjamin Singleton had risked his life helping smuggle slaves to freedom. Now he worked to persuade black people to leave the terror of the South. He told them they should move west and homestead with the white settlers. They, too, were now citizens of the United States and could have their own quarter sections. People listened

Benjamin Singleton was a black leader who persuaded many of his people to leave the South and go homesteading in Kansas. He testified before Congress to explain how black men suffered in the South after the Civil War.

to Benjamin Singleton, and thousands of them even followed his advice.

Homesteading was harder for black settlers than for white. Most of them were too poor to own a covered wagon or even to pay for train fare out west. White Southern farmers did not want them to go — they wanted black people to stay and work for them. Some white Southerners went to great lengths to prevent blacks from leaving. Railroads and boat lines were forbidden to sell tickets to black people. Some who tried to travel were arrested for being vagrants. The leaders who came south to tell people about homesteading were horsewhipped and driven away. Settlers who later went back to get their families were often beaten or killed. More than one black man who returned to the South to get his wife had to steal her as if she were still a slave.

Southern politicians, who were mostly Democrats, decided that it was all a Republican plot. They said that Republicans were paying black people to move west so that they would vote Republican. Congress investigated the whole matter, and Benjamin Singleton went to Washington to testify. He told the congressmen that schools were burned and children made to work in the cotton fields. He told how men's lives were threatened. He told Congress why black people wanted to escape from the South.

Those black people who were able to escape did not always find that they were welcome in the West. Sometimes black settlers were driven away by white settlers. One hundred and fifty black people who came from Mississippi to Lincoln, Nebraska, were chased out of town. Black settlers who went to Denver, Colorado, found that no one would rent houses to them.

But black people still felt the West was better than the South.

This black family homesteaded in Nebraska. The family built a sod house and a sod barn for the animals. To the right of the picture above are the farm horses. At the left is a grindstone used for sharpening axes, sickles, and other farm tools. The roof of the house is made of sod laid over a wood frame. Stovepipes stick up through the roof to carry away the smoke from cooking. The photograph below was taken a few months later. The family have whitewashed their sod house. -

They organized groups to migrate, they pooled their savings, they helped each other. Fifteen thousand poured into Kansas in 1879. They were known as Exodusters. In patched and tattered clothing, with their belongings tied up in bundles, they came upriver on Missouri steamboats. They set about taking out homestead claims and putting up sod houses. Many of the women went to work in the local towns as house servants until their husbands had built houses for the family. Then the wife sometimes stayed on the claim while her husband went to work on the railroad or in a coal mine. The wife and children took care of the small vegetable garden or corn crop until the father made enough money to come home again. Black families helped each other, and sympathetic white people helped too. Before the Civil War there had been only 627 black people in all of Kansas. Fifty years later there were 54,000.

Black settlers went to all the Western states. During the 1870's, 100,000 moved to Texas. In the 1880's, black students were graduating from Nebraskan high schools and serving in the state legislature.

One solution black people had found in Nebraska was to set up all-black towns. There black people could live in peace without being afraid of white people. Many whites preferred not to live in the same town as black people. This same answer worked in other states.

In Oklahoma, twenty-six black towns were set up. Boley was one of these towns. The settlement began as a place where trains stopped for water and for the crews to rest. The man in charge of the train stop was black. Other people came to join him, to live in Boley with him. By the early 1900's, the town had a population of four thousand — all black. The town had water, electricity, and a telephone system. Schools went from the elementary level to junior college. The local newspaper appealed to blacks to come from all over the South: "Come and help us . . . solve the great racial problem that is now before us."

Even in Boley, however, the black settlers found they were not entirely free. They could vote to elect their own city council, but when they tried to take part in county politics they were stopped. White men from other towns refused to sit down with the men from Boley. The county election board refused to accept results from Boley. White settlers all over Oklahoma decided they did not want black people to be equal. A law was passed to stop black people from voting in state elections. The law said that a man could vote only if his grandfather had been a voter. The grandfathers of the black settlers of Boley had been slaves who had not been able to vote. Now their free grandsons could not vote either.

The white farmers around Boley organized and agreed not to let any black men work for them. In a nearby town a white mob killed a black woman and her child.

The dream of black freedom in Oklahoma was dead. But Boley is still a black town where black citizens try to live and work in peace.

Buffalo

Huge herds of big shaggy buffalo roamed all over the Western plains. There may have been as many as seventy million of them when white settlers began moving westward. Early travelers told of riding for days alongside the same big herd. Buffalo wandered slowly, cropping the grass as they went. One herd might take a week to pass any given spot.

Buffalo were not very smart. Their little blinking eyes did not see very far. Their brains moved slowly. But they did not need to be smart. The food they needed, grass, was all around them. They had enemies. Wolves or coyotes attacked their calves. Indians killed them for their meat and their skin. But neither wild animals nor Indians could kill enough buffalo to make any difference to the size of their herds. To the Indians buffalo seemed as endless as the prairie grass.

In the days of the trappers and fur traders even the coming of the white man did not make much difference to the buffalo. The fur traders saw the beautiful robes that the Indian women made from buffalo skins. They bought them from the Indians.

Making a buffalo robe took many weeks of work. After a buffalo had been killed, the women of the tribe carefully stripped off its skin. They stretched the skin out on the ground, flesh side up, and fastened it down with wooden pegs. Then, with sharp bone or stone scrapers, the women scraped off any flesh that was left. If a skin was just left out in the sun to dry, it became hard and brittle. The women kept the skin wet with water in which buffalo brains had been soaked. They rubbed the skin every day

In the early days of the railroads, trains were often held up by herds of buffalo. Travelers amused themselves by shooting buffalo from the train.

for ten days so that it would be soft. When they were finished, the skin was soft and supple, with warm, silky fur.

Both the Indians and traders liked a white buffalo robe best of all. These were very hard to find. Perhaps once in his lifetime a hunter might find an albino buffalo. This is a buffalo born without any color in his fur or his skin or his eyes. His fur is pure white and his eyes are pink. A robe made from an albino buffalo looked like a soft white cloud.

The next most valuable kind of buffalo robe was a "beaver" robe. This did not come from a particular kind of buffalo but was made by the Indian women from any buffalo skin. As they prepared the robe they pulled out the long coarse buffalo hairs, leaving just the short soft hairs so that the buffalo fur looked like beaver fur. Most buffalo were brown but some looked blue or black. These special colors were worth more when the Indians sold them to white traders.

Both white people and Indians loved buffalo robes. Indians wrapped themselves in buffalo robes to keep warm during the long prairie winters. White settlers east and west used buffalo robes as blankets on their beds and to wrap around themselves during long cold rides in sleighs or wagons during the winter. For many years Indians brought their buffalo robes to trading posts to exchange them for guns, axes, blankets, and beads. Indians also used buffalo hides — the skins with the fur taken off. Again it was the Indian women who prepared the hides. They skinned the buffalo, scraped off the flesh and the fur. The skins were hung up around a smoky fire to preserve them. These were the skins used to make clothes and tepees.

For many years white men were not interested in buffalo

BISON HUNTING.

Indians hunted buffalo for food and for skins. At first they hunted on foot. Horses made following the herds and hunting much easier. The Indians used spears and bows and arrows to kill the buffalo. Later they traded furs for guns. .

hides. The hides were not strong enough to make the kind of leather the white man wanted.

White men first hunted buffalo for their meat. Settlers used the meat to feed their own families. Railroad companies needed large quantities of meat to feed the men who were laying the tracks. They hired buffalo hunters to hunt for meat.

Buffalo were easy to shoot. They do not see well and their

sense of smell is also bad. Hunters found they could come quite close to a herd on foot. They could even shoot buffalo without frightening the whole herd into running away. A hunter looked over the herd carefully and decided which was the buffalo leader. He shot the leader first. Without a leader the other buffalo just stood there and the hunter could shoot as many as he wanted to. A hunter one day reported that he fired ninety-one times and killed seventy-six buffalo. He stopped because his arm was tired.

There seemed to be so many buffalo and they were so easy to shoot that men were wasteful. Often hunters took only the best parts of a buffalo carcass and left the rest to rot on the prairie. Buffalo tongues were considered a delicacy. Sometimes a hunter would take only the tongue and leave the rest of the buffalo.

Even with all the killing for meat and for robes there were still countless buffalo, but about 1870 white men found a way to treat buffalo skins to make good leather. Buffalo-skin coats became popular in Europe. That was the beginning of the end for the buffalo. The rush was on. Hundreds of buffalo hunters arrived on the plains to make quick money. Some hunters worked alone, but many came as part of a big outfit. Wagons loaded with hunters and skinners arrived in good hunting areas. These hunters could surround a buffalo herd and shoot hundreds of poor stupid buffalo. First came the hunters shooting. Then in came the skinners. Lines of wagons moved off loaded with buffalo skins. Behind them they left piles of buffalo bodies to rot in the hot prairie sun.

The Indians looked on in dismay. Their buffalo were disappearing. How could they feed their families? How could they build tepees for them? How could they find buffalo robes to keep them warm? How could they get buffalo skins for clothes?

The Indians tried to drive the buffalo hunters away. Again and again they attacked the wagon trains. They killed the hunters. They scalped them. They tortured them to frighten them off. The buffalo hunters had the United States Army to protect them. The federal government was as determined to protect the buffalo hunters as the settlers. The army was delighted to see the buffalo being killed. They knew that with the buffalo gone the Indians would starve.

In fifteen years, millions of buffalo were killed. All over the Great Plains lay dead buffalo. Wolves and coyotes ate the meat. Vultures swooped down and feasted. Insects took their share. What was left stank and rotted in the sun. Soon nothing was left but piles of white and shining bones.

The white man found another use for the buffalo. Bones were worth money. The chemicals in them were used in treating cane sugar. Bones were ground up and used for fertilizer. They were also used to make fine china.

The bone rush was on. Homesteaders short of cash took their wagons and collected buffalo bones. They brought their wagonloads of bones to the railroad towns, where dealers bought them for six dollars a ton.

Bones were stacked up beside the railroads to be shipped east. Piles of bones, as high as a house and a mile long, lay waiting for the trains. In some places they were piled up waiting for the railroad to be built.

Men made fortunes from buffalo bones. Many a prairie farmer was able to feed his family and save his homestead by selling a crop of bones long before he had a crop of wheat ready for market. Even Indians collected and sold buffalo bones to buy food from the white man.

In a few years the bones were collected and almost the last traces of the buffalo were gone from the plains. In 1883 a museum expedition traveling through the West to prepare a display of stuffed buffalo could find fewer than two hundred buffalo. The hunters had done their work well. Twenty years before, there had been millions of buffalo roaming wild and free. Now there were perhaps four thousand left.

To the Indians of the Great Plains the end of the buffalo meant the end of their food supply, the end of their way of life.

Cowboys and Cattlemen

Not all the men who went west wanted to raise corn or wheat. The wide, grassy prairies that suited the buffalo so well were also good for the cattle the settlers brought with them. Land that was too dry for farming was good for cattle. In 1850 there were 330,000 head of cattle in Texas. Ten years later there were ten times as many. All over the West there were millions of acres of empty land. There were few settlers in Colorado, Montana, or the Dakotas. Cattlemen ran their cattle on the open range, letting them feed wherever there was grass. The cattle were rounded up once a year for branding. The owner of the cattle burned his brand, the special mark he used, on his cattle. The cattle then ran free again until the time came to drive them to market.

About 2,500 cattle were rounded up for each drive. Twelve cowboys drove the herd 10 or 15 miles a day for hundreds of miles across the dusty plain. Cowboys and cattle headed for Abilene or Dodge City or another railroad stop.

The cattle trails were laid out from water hole to water hole. The cowboys worked hard, watching the cows and steers night and day. Cattle are both nervous and stupid. A sudden noise could start a stampede with all the cattle racing away. Cowboys had to watch where the cattle were going. If cows came to a cliff, they were likely to walk over if no one headed them off.

Cowboys had a hot, hard, dusty life, but being a cowboy was one way that a man who had nothing could get started in the West. Many men who had learned to ride a horse and shoot a gun

Dodge City was a wild place when cowboys drove a herd of Texas long-horns into town. The cowboys used long whips to control the cattle. They could crack those whips so that they sounded like pistol shots.

during the Civil War went out west to become cowboys. There had been slave cowboys before the war in Texas. After the war, many black men went west as cowboys. About a quarter of all the cowboys who rode the range in the great days of the cattle drive were black. The first man shot in Dodge City was a black cowboy. The first man arrested in Abilene was black.

To the people back east the cowboy became the most popular hero of the West. Thousands of stories were written about their adventures. Many of these stories were about "Deadwood Dick" whose real name was Nat Love and who had been born a slave.

Cowboys rode around the herd at night to guard the cattle. Often they sang songs to keep the cattle quiet. There was always danger that the cattle might become frightened and stampede.

Spirited cowboys arrive in town for a holiday celebration.

The real Nat Love ended up as a Pullman porter on a luxury train, shining shoes for white travelers.

When homesteaders started settling on the open range the cattlemen did not like it. They called the homesteaders nesters or sodbusters. The cattlemen felt they owned all this land over which their cattle roamed. Now in came the homesteaders. These farmers took up land near the best water. They put up fences which stopped the cattle from wandering where they wanted.

The cattlemen fought back. They cut the farmers' fences and

drove their cattle through growing crops. In some places there were wars between sodbusters and cattlemen in which men on both sides were killed.

But the weather did more damage to the cattlemen than to the sodbusters. The summer of 1886 was hot and dry. Water holes emptied. Grass grew brown. Prairie fires broke out and burned up the dry grass. The winter was the worst anyone could remember. Blizzard after blizzard swept across the prairie. The temperature went down to forty-five degrees below zero in Montana. Cattle froze. When the cowboys went out in the spring they found thousands of dead cattle. The day of the open range was gone. Cattlemen bought land and fenced it themselves. The days of the great cattle drives were over too. Cows that walked for hundreds of miles were skinny cows whose meat was tough. Railroads pushed deep into cattle country — cows now rode to market.

The United States Army Moves West

The homesteaders, the cattlemen, the miners, were all moving into the homelands of the Indian tribes, who were not ready to give their homes and hunting grounds to strangers without a battle.

Few white men thought the Indians had a right to defend themselves. Perhaps it was a black man who spoke best for the Indians in Congress. Blanche Kelso Bruce was born a slave. After the Civil War he was elected to the United States Senate. He told the senators: "Our Indian policy and administration seem to me to have been inspired and controlled by a stern selfishness. . . . Indian treaties have generally been made as the condition and instrument of acquiring the valuable territory occupied by the several Indian nations, and have been changed and revised from time to time as it became desirable that the steadily growing, irrepressible white races should secure more room."

Congress did not listen to Senator Bruce or to anyone else who pleaded for the Indians. After 1871, Congress decided not to sign any more treaties with Indian tribes. Indians were not to be treated as members of tribes but as individuals. Since they were not citizens, this left the Indians with no rights at all.

In 1887 Congress passed the Dawes Severalty Act that divided the land on Indian reservations into parcels. Each head of a family was given 160 acres; unmarried adults received 80 acres; and the land left over was sold to non-Indians. At the same time laws were passed forbidding Indians to practice their

Blanche Kelso Bruce was born a slave. During the Civil War he was a servant to his white half-brother. After the war he became a planter in Mississippi and was elected to the United States Senate where he fought for the rights of his own people and of the Indians.

own tribal religions. Most white men in the United States were Christians and many felt that the Indians should become Christians too. Missionaries visited the Indians to persuade them to become Christian, and the United States government tried to help the missionaries.

While Congress was busy passing laws, the Indians of the plains fought on against the white invaders. Where there were no railroads, settlers moving west on foot, on horseback, or by wagon followed trails marked by the wagon wheels of those who had gone before. The government tried to protect the trails along which the settlers and miners moved westward. Before 1871 many treaties were made with Indian tribes for the use of the trails.

Officials offered Indians yearly payments of goods or money.

Drawing of a family being attacked by Indians. The men are shooting while mother and the children hide. Grandmother is bandaging grandfather's arm. Over the fireplace is a candle for light, and the iron which mother heated in the fire before she used it. A cooking pot sits by the fireplace. All the cooking in this cabin would have been done over the open fire. On the floor is a baby's cradle hollowed from a log of wood. Hanging from the rafters is the family wash and a string of onions.

Some tribes agreed. Others feared that the traffic along the trails would frighten away the animals the Indians hunted. They also feared the coming of more white settlers.

There were constant skirmishes between travelers crossing the plains and bands of roving Indians. The army came west to guard the travelers. To army officers one Indian tribe was much the same as any other. Frequently soldiers attacked whatever band of Indians they happened to meet.

For a long time the Sioux in Minnesota felt that they had been cheated in agreements they had made with the United States. In 1862 they went on the warpath. They roamed far and wide, killing farmers and their families in lonely cabins. The uprising was put down and almost all the Indian leaders were executed in a public hanging. Little Crow, the main leader, escaped but was killed by settlers the following year. The memory of the massacre lasted for many years. Settlers and soldiers alike were afraid and were ready to shoot any Indian.

There was fighting in Colorado where the Cheyennes tried to stop miners going into the mountains. A Cheyenne chief, Black Kettle, made peace and led his people into camp at Sand Creek. Soldiers attacked and killed somewhere between 150 and 500 men, women, and children. Fighting broke out all over the West. Indians attacked farms and towns and wagon trains.

The Indians had guns and horses and a brave spirit. They had no way of getting more guns or more ammunition except from the white man. Once the Civil War ended, the United States had a large, modern, and well-trained army to send against the Indians. From 1865 to 1891 the chief task of the United States Army was to fight Indians, to kill them, or to drive them onto reservations. Each year the reservations became smaller, on

Little Crow led his people in the "Minnesota Massacre" of 1862, when many settlers were killed.

poorer and poorer land. "Reservation" usually referred to land that was so poor farmers did not want it.

General William Tecumseh Sherman had been one of the most feared generals of the Civil War. He felt the people of the South would not surrender until they thought their country was being totally destroyed. As his army marched south, his soldiers burned crops and houses and killed all the farm animals they could find.

At the end of the war, Sherman was sent out west to fight Indians. His soldiers again destroyed everything they could. When they raided an Indian camp they burned the tepees and the buffalo robes. They killed Indian children so that they could not grow up to become warriors.

General Sherman talked of a "final solution" to the Indian

After the Sioux uprising in Minnesota, thirty-eight Indians were hanged in Mankato, Minnesota. A large platform was built high off the ground so that everyone could see the hanging. The army stood guard while the citizens of Mankato cheered the execution.

General William Tecumseh Sherman. He saw Indians only as a nuisance in the way of the settling of the West by farmers.

problem — to kill as many Indians as possible. Another Civil War general who went out west to fight Indians said: "The only good Indians I ever saw were dead."

The soldiers who fought the Indians were volunteers. The government drafted young men into the army during the Civil War, but the draft ended as the war ended. Many soldiers wanted to go home to their families. Others, who liked army life, stayed on and became Indian fighters. Many men who thought army life out west sounded like a great adventure became soldiers.

One out of five of all the soldiers who fought in the West was black. During the Civil War, the Northern army had some black regiments, although almost all the officers in the regiment were white. After the war many black men joined the army to escape from the South. The black regiments were sent west — again led by white officers.

The job of all these soldiers, both black and white, was to kill Indians and protect settlers. The soldiers marched with wagon trains. They protected the railroads. Forts were built all over the West where soldiers lived and settlers took shelter during Indian attacks.

Indian Resistance

In the Southwest, Navahos and Apaches fought Spaniards, Texans, and the army across Arizona and New Mexico for many years. Colonel Kit Carson defeated the Navahos and drove them onto an arid reservation. The Apaches held out for many years longer. Their leaders, such as Geronimo and Cochise, were some of the most famous of all the Indian chiefs who fought for their people's freedom. Small bands of Apaches hid in the rocky hills of the Southwest, sweeping out to attack army units. Apache resistance did not end until Geronimo surrendered in 1886.

When the army captured an Indian leader or a group of Indians, it liked to send its prisoners to some faraway spot. Geronimo was imprisoned in Florida.

Geronimo tried to help his people escape from the barren reservation on which the army had placed them. The photograph at the top was taken in 1886, the year of his surrender. The painting below, made eleven years later, shows Geronimo as a defeated old man.

Chief Joseph and the Nez Percés

Where the states of Washington, Oregon, and Idaho meet there are high hills, green valleys, and fast-running streams. About five thousand Indians lived there. They were known as the Nez Percés. This name had been given to them by French trappers. When the French first met them, it was the fashion among the Indians to wear a shell ornament in their noses. The French called them Nez Percés, which means pierced noses. Even when fashion changed and the Nez Percés no longer wore shells in their noses, the name remained.

The Nez Percés lived in small villages scattered through the hills. Most of them lived along the banks of rivers where they caught fish.

In the early eighteenth century the Nez Percés had raided the camps of their enemies the Shoshoni and captured their horses. The Nez Percés bred these horses until they had a spotted horse called the Appaloosa that could run far and fast. On their beautiful horses they rode out across the plains to hunt buffalo. They carried with them their bows made from the horns of mountain sheep. Always they came back to their villages in the green hills.

The Nez Percés had many friendly contacts with white men. They did business with the French and British fur traders who came down from Canada. Some of their young men went back to Canada with the fur traders to go to school. Other young men were sent across the wide plains to the Missouri River to buy guns. The Nez Percés became so interested in the white man's way of life that they invited missionaries to come and live among them and teach them about the white man's god.

In 1855 the Nez Percé chiefs signed a treaty with the United States government. The treaty guaranteed that a large piece of land would be set aside as a reservation on which the Nez Percés could live.

The years of peace in the green hills soon ended, however. In 1860 a white man found gold on Nez Percé land and miners flocked in. Noisy mining towns grew up. In 1863 the United States government again sent men to visit the Nez Percés. They redrew the boundaries of the reservation, making it much smaller. Some of the chiefs agreed, but others did not sign. The days of the Nez Percés as free men were numbered. Settlers continued to move in. The federal government tried to make room for the settlers by moving the Nez Percés onto an even smaller reservation.

In the Wallowa River Valley of Oregon lived a band of Nez Percés with their chief, Joseph. Homesteaders moved into the area. Chief Joseph and his people were ordered to move onto the reservation. Although they did not want to leave their home in the valley they loved, they agreed to go.

At the same time some settlers in Idaho were killed by Indians. The soldiers decided, as they often did, that all Indians were dangerous. Although the soldiers did not know exactly who had killed the settlers, they attacked Chief Joseph and his Nez Percés. The Indians fought back. Other bands of Nez Percés joined them. The whole group decided not to go onto the reservation. Instead, they decided to try to leave the United States and go to Canada. There they felt they might be able to live in peace and freedom. They set off on a long march through the moun-

Chief Joseph led his people, a band of the Nez Percé Indians, in their struggle against the United States. The artist has shown him in a feathered warbonnet although Joseph was not a war chief and few Indians ever wore warbonnets.

tains of Idaho and Montana. For 1,300 miles they struggled on — men, women, and children. The soldiers followed, mile after mile. Again and again the Nez Percés had to stop and fight the soldiers. They almost reached Canada. The soldiers attacked once more. For five days the Nez Percés fought. Chief Joseph finally surrendered, saying: "Hear me, my chiefs, I am tired; my heart is sick and sad. From where the sun now stands, I will fight no more forever."

The Nez Percés who had fought the white man were sent far

away to Oklahoma. Chief Joseph did not give up. He pleaded with the federal government to let the Nez Percés go back to their homeland. He traveled to Washington, D.C., to speak to the nation's politicians. He said: "If the white man wants to live in peace with the Indian he can live in peace. . . . Treat all men alike. Give them all the same law. Give them all an even chance to live and grow. All men were made by the same Great Spirit Chief. They are all brothers. The earth is the mother of all people, and all people should have equal rights upon it. . . . Let me be a free man — free to travel, free to stop, free to work, free to trade where I choose, free to choose my own teachers, free to follow the religion of my fathers, free to think and act for myself — and I will obey the law or submit to the penalty."

Chief Joseph and his people were never allowed to return to their own Wallowa Valley. -

The War Goes On

Red Cloud, a chief of the Oglala Sioux, did not want white men traveling the lands on which his tribe roamed. He became one of the few Indians ever to force the United States Army to withdraw from land it had occupied.

A trail was mapped out, running from the Platte River to the mines in Montana. Red Cloud refused to sign a treaty allowing white men to travel along the trail. The government sent troops in to build forts to protect the trail.

Red Cloud and his braves attacked the troops as they moved in. The forts were built, but Indians attacked the soldiers as they came and went from their forts. When a large group of soldiers went out to gather firewood for the winter, Red Cloud and his men ambushed them. Many of the soldiers were killed.

The constant Indian raids made it impossible for travelers to use the trail. The soldiers withdrew. The forts were abandoned. Red Cloud had won a victory for his tribe. He signed a peace treaty with the United States government. This treaty guaranteed that the Black Hills of South Dakota would be part of a large reservation set aside for the Sioux. These Black Hills were held sacred by the Indians. Some of their most important religious ceremonies were held there.

The Black Hills were not sacred to white men — and especially not to one white man named George Custer. He was a handsome young man and a successful one. Custer was used to having his own way and did not often think about things that were important to other people.

Red Cloud and his men. He was one of the few Indians who were able to force the United States Army to withdraw, if only for a time. It was in the West that Indian chiefs wore the great feathered warbonnets.

Custer's soldiers are setting out through the snow to attack an Indian village.

After the Civil War, Custer was sent west to fight Indians. He had no high opinion of treaties or Indians or anyone who tried to stop him from doing what he wanted to do. He was looking for gold in the Black Hills — his troops marched in and found it. Custer spread the news, and miners poured into the holy hills of the Sioux.

The federal government offered to buy the Black Hills from the Indians. But the Sioux could not think of selling sacred ground. The government ordered the Sioux to leave the Black Hills. They were to go to other reservations set aside for them.

The Sioux fought back, led by two of their greatest chiefs, Crazy Horse and Sitting Bull. Crazy Horse defeated the United States Army at Rosebud Creek. Custer moved on, seeking to punish the Indians. Crazy Horse and Sitting Bull met him at the Little Big Horn. Custer was killed and so were his men.

That was the last great victory ever won by Indians. Custer had been popular. His handsome face and long blond hair had been known all over the country. Everywhere white men demanded that his defeat be avenged.

The United States Army was determined to defeat the In-

"Custer's Death Struggle." The artist who drew this picture has shown General Custer dressed in his parade uniform. Pictures like this helped to make people think of General Custer as a great hero and of the Indians as terrible savages. The battle at Little Big Horn lasted about an hour. More than two hundred soldiers were killed.

dians once and for all. Sitting Bull fled with his people to Canada. Crazy Horse was imprisoned and killed. Some of the Cheyenne Indians, who had fought with the Sioux, were rounded up and sent hundreds of miles away to a reservation in Oklahoma. There they were unhappy and homesick. In 1878 they escaped and set off on the long march to their homeland in the north country. Federal soldiers chased them and killed most of them.

The Last Battle

By 1889 the Indians were subdued. Most of them were living on reservations. The buffalo were gone. Many Indians had been killed by bullets and disease.

That year a young Indian named Wovoka fell ill. He had a dream. In the dream God spoke to him, telling him that all men should love one another and be brothers. If they did, they would meet their friends again in the other world after death.

Wovoka told his people of the dream. He also told them of a dance. The religion of the Indians had always included dancing as a form of worship. Wovoka taught his people the "ghost dance." Hundreds of Indians danced for many days, going without food or water. Many dancers fell to the ground in a trance, seeing visions of the days of old. They dreamed again of the great herds of buffalo, of galloping across the wide plains, of the days of Indian power and glory.

Tribes all over the plains heard of the ghost dance. Many men traveled to Nevada where Wovoka lived to talk with him. They carried the story of the ghost dance back to their tribes. All over the West, Indians began gathering by the hundreds to dance.

White settlers were nervous. They did not understand why the Indians were gathering. They asked the government to send more soldiers.

Sitting Bull had come back from Canada. He was the most famous Indian in the United States. After the Little Big Horn he was the Indian whom white men feared most. As the settlers became more and more upset, soldiers decided to arrest Sitting

Indians gathered together to dance the "ghost dance." They dreamed of the days when they had lived in peace and there were plenty of buffalo for everyone. The army feared an uprising and rushed to arrest Indian leaders.

Bull, the man they felt was most likely to lead an uprising. Traitorous Indians who worked for the white man were sent to Sitting Bull's cabin. They walked in while he was still asleep. They woke him up and told him to come with them.

"I am not going," said Sitting Bull, and they shot him. Crow Foot, his seventeen-year-old son, was also shot.

When the Sioux saw their great leader dead, all hope left

them. Most of them began to go back to the reservations where the white man wanted them. A group gathered around Chief Big Foot, who was ill with pneumonia in the bitter winter weather.

The soldiers decided to arrest Big Foot. Three thousand went out to round up the chief and his followers. The soldiers marched Big Foot with his cold and hungry people to Wounded Knee Creek, where the Indians set up their tepees in the snow.

The sick chief and his people were left alone. Then, on the morning of December 29, 1890, the soldiers marched to the camp and surrounded it. The order was given for the Indians to give

Sitting Bull led his warriors against General Custer at the Battle of the Little Big Horn. He escaped with many of his people to Canada. Later he came back to the United States. He was killed by soldiers who came to arrest him at the time when the army feared that the "ghost dancers" were about to lead an armed revolt.

No. 3605. Indian Chiefs and U. S. Officials.
1 Two Strike. 6 Kicking Bear. 12 W. F. Cody, (Buf-
            falo Bill)
2 Crow Dog. 7 Good Voice. 13 Maj. J M. Burk.
3 Short Bull. 8 Thunder Hawk. 14 J. C. Craiger.
4 High Hawk. 9 Rocky Bear. 15 J. McDonald.
5 Two Lance. 10 Young man afraid 16 J. G. Worth
            of his horse.
            11 American Horse.
Taken at Pine Ridge Jan. 16. '91. Photo and copyright
        by Grabill, 1891, Deadwood, S. D.

Indians chiefs met with United States officials many times during the years of the Indian wars to try to work out terms for peace. These men met at Pine Ridge, South Dakota, in January, 1891. Before the year was over the massacre at Wounded Knee ended Indian resistance..

up their arms. The soldiers marched into the camp to look for guns. They walked into the tepees. They poked and prodded. They threw the Indians' blankets and clothes all over the ground. They hunted for guns everywhere. The women and children were scared and the Indian men were angry. Yellow Bird, a medicine man who was watching, was also angry. He shouted to the men around him and told them the ghost dance had given them strength. He told them that the magic of the dance had made their shirts bulletproof. As a signal to his people, Yellow Bird hurled a handful of earth into the air. A shot rang out.

The soldiers were ready. They fired into the crowd. The guns they carried were repeater rifles that could fire again and again without being reloaded. Indian men, women, and children fell dead in the snow. The soldiers ran after those who tried to escape and killed them.

This was the last great battle the United States Army fought against the Indians — this killing in the snow at Wounded Knee. Almost all the Indians died — more than two hundred people. Sixty-two of the dead were women and children. Twenty-nine white men were killed. The bodies lay in the snow and froze.

Indian resistance was over after almost four hundred years. The white man was in control of the whole country of the United States from sea to shining sea. The army had no trouble rounding up stray Indians and herding them onto reservations.

The End of the Frontier

By 1900 there were settlers in most areas of the West. The United States had nearly three times as many farms as forty years before. More than two times as many acres were being farmed. These new farms produced food to be shipped to the large cities. Less than one-fifth of the people of the United States lived in the new areas, but half the sheep, wheat, and cattle in the whole country came from there.

Millions of acres were still empty — and available for homesteading — but most of that was dry and barren. Indeed, men were to find that many of the homesteaders had moved onto land that was too dry for farming. Once the sod had been broken, and the land plowed, many farmers found that a few dry years turned their farms to dust that blew away on the prairie winds.

From the beginning this had been a land where settlers had moved westward over the mountains and across the plains. Now the United States was different from what it had ever been before. There were no more large stretches of fertile land to settle. Men in eastern cities or in Europe could no longer dream of a farm in the West.

Indians could dream only of the past. The white man had won the long war. -

Index